Ninja Virgin

First published 2025 by The Hedgehog Poetry Press,

5 Coppack House, Churchill Avenue, Clevedon. BS21 6QW

www.hedgehogpress.co.uk

Copyright © Fiona Pitt-Kethley 2025

The right of Fiona Pitt-Kethley to be identified as the author of this work has been asserted in accordance with the Copyright, Designs and Patents Act 1988. All rights reserved. No part of this publication may be reproduced, stored in or introduced into a retrieval system, or transmitted in any form, or by any means (electronic, mechanical, photocopying, recording or otherwise) without prior written permissions of the publisher. Any person who does any unauthorised act in relation to this publication may be liable for criminal prosecution and civil claims for damages.

ISBN: 978-1-916830-42-4

Ninja Virgin

by

Fiona Pitt-Kethley

Contents

Ninja Virgin 6
Invocation 8
My Kind of Saints 9
Jonah 10
Synchronised Swimming 11
The Garden of Earthly Delights 12
Talking at Once 13
My Lucky Cat 14
Hill-Walking 15
Ferret Parties of Cartagena 16
The Illuminati 17
PTSD 18
Prayer to the Lares and Penates 19
The Third Way 20
Unfinished Stories 21
Troupers 22
Circuses 23
Eunuch 24
Our Lady of the Port 25
Ruta 66 26

Acknowledgements 28

NINJA VIRGIN

She wraps her form in black instead of blue.
Everything's covered, shoes are flexible.
Her halo's in her backpack, zipped away.

The job is on. She climbs a block of flats.
Cuts glass using her diamond laser nails,
enters the bedroom where a sick child sleeps.
Somebody prayed? It's Ninja Virgin here.
Puts halo on. Time for a miracle.
The child turns in her sleep and starts to sweat.
Next day the doctor'll say the crisis passed.

Now Ninja Virgin's gone. She abseils down.
Crosses the busy road, picks up a dog,
that almost went beneath a taxi's wheels.
The driver sees the dog up in the air
but not the Ninja Virgin holding him.
He hits the brakes and skids but halts in time.
She's off. Another job. A homeless man
lies on the sidewalk in his tattered rags.
His head is pillowed on a bag of clothes.
A filthy blanket covers most of him.
No priest around to give him the last rites.
He sees her, smiles, says. "Mary!" as he dies.
She can't save everyone. That's not her brief.
The police will find him by the morning's light.
She's closed his eyes to hide their ecstasy.

She's at the hospital. The doors swing wide.
She's only visible to those like her:
night people, loners, those who're on the edge.
The porter winks at her. She's in the ward,
unhooking oxygen, breathing her life
into the old ones fighting for each breath.
Doctors and nurses check the monitors.
A power-cut perhaps. But all is fine.
Pulses are checked. Some mini miracles.
But none acknowledged by the men of science.

It's almost morning now. She's off again
to hide her darkness from the coming light.
Her black would be no camouflage at all.
She's worked her shift. It's time for morning saints.

INVOCATION

At the start of February, I found
a casserole abandoned on the beach.
Inside it was a tangled mess of things:
snail shells, a doll's head, cotton-wool and cloth,
a mirror, photo, name and lock of hair.
Nearby, some fruit was floating in the sea.

My occult reading led me to believe
this was a curse. I searched the woman's name,
contacted her by email to report.
An out of office answer came straight back,
mentioning her absence was on medical leave.

Next day, a different answer said a friend
would contact and explain it all to me.

Santeria gets a bad press in most films.
Practitioners are labelled psychopaths.
The one who contacted seemed likeable.
This rite, he said, was simply one for health.
The goddess, Yemaja, was being invoked.

I put the dish back in the sea next day,
round in a spot that was less visible
to prying beachcombers who scavenge there.

Somehow the seascape is forever changed.
The sky and water seem a deeper blue.
I feel the presence there of something else:
the Stella Maris of a pagan world,
a mother goddess from another time.

MY KIND OF SAINTS

I like the ones that rescued animals.
Helping the poor and sick is also fine.
I hate the ones that went in for self-harm,
chopped off their bollocks rather than resist,
or pulled their eyes out, set them on a plate

Learned is good. St. Isidore displayed
encyclopaedic knowledge in his books.
And Hildegard made music of the spheres.

Religion gives all saints a second life.
They can be prayed to like the Pagan Gods,
or else become an intermediary,
like minor office staff going to the Boss.
St. Anthony, most popular of them all,
for finding stuff, a really useful saint.

JONAH

A whale-tail sculpture close to the port side
commemorates one that was stranded there.
Sometimes the winter brings reports of deaths:
a whale, a shark, a porpoise on a beach.
Just once, I saw a pod of dolphins pass.

These days they have post-mortems to decide,
cut open carcasses retrieved from shores.
No prophets in the bellies of these whales,
but something else that spells our future doom,
entrails stuffed hard with plastic from the waves.
The plankton cocktail's laced with deadly bits
that gradually entangle to a mass
and choke the creature's life from inside out.

SYNCHRONISED SWIMMING

The TV in the bar has sound turned down.
No music to explain the funky walk
the squad of eight enjoys beside the pool.
Nymphs channelling the android that's within.
Costumes that almost seem spray-painted on.
Nothing is natural about these dolls.
Their hair is always brown, lacquered to their heads,
topped by a little bun pinned with brocade.
Their make-up's built to last through Noah's flood.

Amphibious cheerleaders, identical
as octuplets born from a factory womb.
Take one out on a date. They're all the same,
with nose-pegs always perfectly in place
flashing a special forty-tooth white smile.
Hard to imagine life beyond the pool.

They're in and lashing like a group of sharks,
upside-down spinning followed by flailing legs.
Their older fatter Mums along the edge
 applaud each move, ooze pride from every pore.

THE GARDEN OF EARTHLY DELIGHTS

I mostly swim quite early in the day.
There's space. The bay is almost empty then.
One night, hoping to see the Perseids we went
just before sundown to enjoy this scene.
As usual I swam out to the barrier
as I came back the light was fading fast,
the beach was packed with partying families,
small groups and clusters, lighting barbecues,
some well-equipped, others with coals on rocks,
fanning the flames, hoping to cook a feast.
Inflatables of every type and shape
beached from the sea, were drawn up here and there,
rings, horses, unicorns and blow-up chairs.
Something about the grouping of this scene
reminded me of Bosch. All life was there.

We lay back on the shingle, searched the dark,
shutting out all the busy scene around.
Clouds parted; tiny stars flashed through the sky.

TALKING AT ONCE

Talking at once, a very Spanish thing.
It's easy to despair and get no grasp,
until you see it as an orchestra.
It's necessary to know some people there.
X is intelligent with lots to give,
Y frequently just spouts a load of shit.
Watch carefully, select a voice to hear...
Pick out the melody, block out the rest.
Move from the flute and try a violin,
on to bassoons but leave the timpani.

MY LUCKY CAT

My lucky cat waves at me through the day.
Supposed to bring in wealth, it brings in none.
You'd think that I would know the score by now.
I've been through many so-called lucky charms.
The Lincoln Imp brought me so much ill luck
eventually I left it on a bench.
Its devilish smirk could lure some other fool.

Why do I bother? Hard to analyse.
Like those who pray and keep their powder dry,
when keeping powder dry might be enough...

Logic might say talent and work's enough,
And yet there is another element.
X is successful, Y a never-was.
Z has some luck but loses it again.
Reality shows that there's something else.
Not what you know but who you know some say.
Yet, even that, simplifies things too much.
These pixies, lucky cats, MIGHT have a role,
might give an edge where work and talent fail.

HILL-WALKING

As I walk, I aim for the mountain-top
and keep going whatever gets in my way.
I am not allowed to rest till I get there.
There is a lesson to be learned on high,
something you can't know on the lower roads.
When you are at the crest, then you can see
the other side. No hint of that below.
The light is always different on that side.
One part of a mountain can be happy
and the other sad. One can be clothed in plants.
Sheep or goats might graze there. Sometimes, also,
there are hidden mysteries in the folds
of a mountain, valleys, ponds, ruined houses
that tell me of a past lost history.
The message from the mountain runs like this:
there are always two sides to every question;
all obstacles are there to be surpassed
and what is beyond is unknowable
until you get there and experience it.

FERRET PARTIES OF CARTAGENA

They meet each Wednesday by the city walls,
a dozen or so, students caretaking them

Fat-bellied youngsters, lying on their backs,
males with their pale-pink penises exposed
showing debauched rake's-progress kind of looks,
sweet shyer females running on the grass.

I learn a little of their urban life
and how they integrate with other pets.
A ferret can give a rather nasty bite
and gets depressed if it's not entertained.
Some live with rabbits and a fox in town.
The fox is gentle, also goes for walks.
One ferret uses children's parks at night
and chuckles as she slithers down the slide.

THE ILLUMINATI

An intellectual movement of its day,
spread throughout Europe until banned
Perhaps they were the only real ones,
Goethe was definitely one of them,
Mozart, perhaps, Beethoven, so they say...
The first Illuminati had a role
tempting the queen to buy a necklace.
Enough to bring the Revolution on,
some parts of which were good and needed then.
Yet Revolutions go from bad to worse
Nothing stays put, like rivers to the sea,
Just and unjust are swept away in time.

Nobody ever called them lizards then,
magicians sometimes, always human though.
In urban legends they are always bad,
rich families out to control the world.
Perhaps they're just movers behind the scenes,
Asking right questions at the perfect time,
Tumbling the Berlin Wall or opening jails
to let out those imprisoned wrongfully.

What do we have against them? Secrecy?
But secrecy is good in charity,
No boasting, vaunting, using it for tax,
the widow's mite, the rich man's fortune too.
And secrecy is good until a plan
is fully fledged rather than just half-formed.

PTSD

"We shall remember them" ...No, not the dead,
the maimed, the visibly scarred ones we see.
I speak of the men who came back damaged.
Whose lives were changed by what they saw or felt,
the horrors that they could not leave behind.

Those who can't sleep, who wake up in the night
remembering, who leave their families.
Those who can't hold an average job by day.
Everything's changed for them. It's not the same.
These heroes who sleep now on pavements,
who are moved on by police and shuffle off,
carrying all possessions in a bag,
living in the line of fire, forever,
unable to forget or come to terms.
These heroes fought for us and we failed them.
No medals for this other kind of death.

PRAYER TO THE LARES AND PENATES

My German great grandfather who decamped
leaving a Bristol girl to raise his child.
And Harriet Richens, an abandoned girl,
in turn passed on her kid for bringing up,
no birth certificate, but cash enough
to hide her kid and be respectable.
My Gran, mistreated, was soon snatched away
brought up in place of one who died when young.
Harriet lost contact soon and that was that.

My father's parents didn't approve his wife.
Didn't attend the wedding at the time.
His mother died of shock at losing her son.
I have one photo to remember her,
a picture from her youth, sisters beside.
Ellen Reed looked slightly Victorian
A woman who died years before I was born.
A distant relative traced her descent
from pilots based in Pill, some of whom drowned,
a teacher named Bathsheba in Corfu.

My grandfather, a widower, came around
and entertained my parents for a while.
A rich but stingy man when Christmas came
he sank a crate of champagne on his own.
Not wasting it on sons or daughter-in-law.
After his death, his cash bought us a house.

Part of my past, in some sense family
those other ones who kept away from us.
They chose a separation from the rest.
I call on my dead family to help,
especially the ones that didn't in life.

THE THIRD WAY

There's always a third path, sometimes a fourth.

Watching the Matrix...The red pill or blue....
I think I'd choose to send them both away,
while someone else might think he'd hazard both.

And is the glass half empty or half full?
Who cares? It's what they put inside that counts
and whether others have a larger glass

Multiple choice in questions offers four,
but rarely those I'd really like to choose.
Quizzes and crosswords settle for a choice
that's always over simple in intent

Yes, no, or maybe, and a thousand shades
exist in life. No black or white out there.
Colours are far less absolute than this
and so is life. A thousand ways to go.

UNFINISHED STORIES

The world is full of unfinished stories.
There was the cow's skeleton and sleeping bag
side by side in a ruined foundry.
There were concrete gateposts sculpted as trees
each side of a gate that's always closed.
There was the man with a scythe out walking
with a lady in slippers and dressing-gown behind.
There was a man carrying a cockerel in Cartagena.
Tail feathers protruding from his djellaba
soon gave the game away as did the noise.
He was leaving an area of cock fights and drugs.
Was he saving the bird for soup or life
crowing on its own dunghill somewhere else.
There was the rainbow unicorn's horn on a band
left overnight upon my window-sill

TROUPERS

I like to watch an old performer play
not just a pretty face, the transience
of someone who's attractive for a while,
rewarded for this rather than their art.
Experience, many decades of it.
Think yourself lucky when you see an act
that's old. Catch them before they die,
taking their wit and wisdom to the grave.

Sometimes I'm sad for their fragility.
Do they crave rest? Maybe they do at times.
And yet, giving their talent to the world
beats rotting in an average Old Folks' home
These stars burn brightly to their very end.

Omara Portuondo singing on,
her face still beautiful, her body slow,
reminds me that there's hope for all of us.
Eighty-three and she's telling the world "So what!"
Her band, who're not exactly in the flush
of youth, are calling her the sexiest.
Young singers kiss her, celebrate her style,
A tribute to the permanence of art.

CIRCUSES

I showed my son a Roman theatre
when he was six. His eyes were wide as I
explained what sort of shows the Romans liked.
My husband commented that tastes had changed,
few now could stomach watching cruelty.

Time to go home and son politely asked
to see a Christian eaten by a lion...

EUNUCH

Hadim stands naked in an alleyway.
His nipples droop, his fists are lightly clenched.
A Sally Army woman and a child,
in fluffy carpet slippers, stare at him.
His eyes are level, almost challenging,
as he displays the scar between his legs.

For weeks, I kept his photo in a drawer,
then wrote a note to the photographer.
I had to know the story of his life.

By Turkish law, penis and testicles
had been lopped off. He'd raped a girl of six.
Twenty years past, the punishment goes on…
His sentence keeps him naked as a babe.
The only mercy that's allowed to him,
a turban to protect his head from sun,
which in that climate could cause premature death.

I told the story at a summer barbecue.
Most of the men remarked: "Good show!" and thought
that child-abusers all should get the chop.
Hadim, of course, was never a nice man
and quite unlike the sort of men they knew.

The alley's wet with a rare shower of rain.
He stands alone, a living monument,
Don Juan's Commendatore, still in Hell,
exudes a kind of damaged dignity.
He doesn't see the crowd, looks past at us,
ignores the other little girl of six.
The question that he seems to ask is this:
"Twenty years on, victim or criminal,
which of us has been healed by Time, and which
portrays Man's inhumanity to Man?"

OUR LADY OF THE PORT

Street cleaners, Guardia, workers from the fields
all breakfast here, making an early start.
Sometimes she visits in a gauzy Basque,
long coat in winter, skirt slit to the thigh.
She's clocking off just as they're clocking on.
The men. some clients perhaps, all joke with her.
Did she have breakfast of another kind?
And could they swipe credit cards down her butt?
She laughs at this and doesn't seem to mind.
She drinks her coffee laced with a liqueur
and takes a brandy chaser on the side.
Sometimes buys cigarettes from the machine.
Takes home some water and a madeleine.
Departs perchance to sleep, perhaps to dream.

RUTA 66

A theme pub, everything's American...
cowboys and Indians, film-stills on the walls.
A blow-up female with no genitals
except some drawn-on ones (cheaper that way)
lies face down on a table meant for pool.
Naff is the adjective that springs to mind
Hardly the sort of place that you'd expect
hauntings and poltergeist activity.
No history that's visible to me.
The pub is modern. It was built just where
a crossroads with a market used to be.
More 666 than sixty-six, this Route,
these days it seems a thoroughfare to hell.

The panel gives a talk – live radio –
shows us invited guests hundreds of slides
and plays recordings of the things they heard.
I know one of the men involved.
He doesn't seem the sort to fake such things,
a decent guy, and yet I'm sceptical.
Unconscious cheats might push a Ouija board,
desperately hoping that the spirits come through,
leaning until it seems that they're at work...

Their cameras picked up a set of images,
some obvious, others vague like dot-to-dot
before a kid's connected it with pen.
A troop of figures bearing lights appears...
Trooping to where? And when and why? I ask.
Passing along a path of past atrocities:
The Civil War, The Inquisition, crimes...
a kind of ley line left by ancient pain.

It's all another way to look at life,
sincerity amongst the panel at the front,
not conscious cheats but eager to believe.
A different way to look out at the world:
Mother Theresa's grinning on a bun,
phantoms appear in every curtain fold.
Childlike imagination still at work.
I half regret I can't see much of this.

ACKNOWLEDGEMENTS

Cover art by Karen Little.

Some of the individual poems have been published in the following; *International Times, Prole, The Seventh Quarry, Vine Leaves, Banshee, Crannog, Ink, Sweat and Tears, Poetry Journal,* and the anthology, *Mother Mary Comes to Me.*